LOVE QUOTES

MEGHA YADAV

Made with ♥ on the Notion Press Platform
www.notionpress.com

Contents

Contents

Contents

Contents

Contents

Chapter1

"Love is like a puzzle. It may take time and patience to piece together, but once it's complete, it's a beautiful work of art."

Chapter2

"True love is when you know someone's flaws and imperfections, but still choose to love them with all your heart."

Chapter3

"Love is not about possession. It's about appreciation, understanding, and accepting the other person for who they are."

Chapter4

"In love, it's not about finding someone who completes you. It's about finding someone who accepts you as you are and makes you want to be a better person."

Chapter5

"When you love someone, you see the beauty in everything. The world becomes a more beautiful place because of them."

Chapter6

"Love is not just a feeling, it's an action. It's choosing to be patient, kind, and supportive every day."

Chapter7

"True love is not about finding someone who is perfect, but about finding someone who is perfect for you."

Chapter8

"Love is not about finding someone to fill a void in your life, but about sharing your happiness and building a life together."

Chapter9

"When you find someone who makes you laugh, smile, and feel alive, hold on to them and never let them go."

Chapter10

"Love is a journey, not a destination. It's about enjoying the ride and making memories along the way."

Chapter11

"Love is like a flame. It can burn brightly and passionately, or it can be gentle and warm. Either way, it brings light to your life."

Chapter12

"True love is not about finding someone who completes you, but about finding someone who accepts you as you are and helps you grow."

Chapter13

"Love is not just a feeling, it's a choice. It's choosing to love someone even when it's difficult, and working together to overcome challenges."

Chapter14

"When you love someone, you don't just love them for their strengths, but also for their vulnerabilities and imperfections."

Chapter15

"Love is not about being perfect, but about being willing to grow and learn together."

Chapter16

"True love is not just about the good times, but also about standing by each other during the hard times."

Chapter17

"When you find someone who makes you feel safe, cherished, and understood, hold on to them and never let go."

Chapter18

"Love is about being present and attentive to the other person. It's about listening, supporting, and caring for them."

Chapter19

"True love is not just about passion, but also about building a deep, lasting connection."

Chapter20

"Love is about creating a home in each other's hearts, a place where you can always come back to and find comfort."

Chapter21

"Love is a language that transcends words. It's communicated through actions, gestures, and the way we look at each other."

Chapter22

"True love is not just about finding someone who shares your interests, but about finding someone who shares your values and vision for the future."

Chapter23

"When you love someone, you don't just see them for who they are now, but for who they have the potential to become."

Chapter24

"Love is about supporting each other's dreams and helping each other achieve them."

Chapter25

"True love is not just about finding someone who makes you happy, but about finding someone who challenges you to be a better person."

Chapter26

"When you love someone, you don't just love the good parts of them, but also the parts that are difficult and challenging."

Chapter27

"Love is about accepting each other's differences and embracing them as part of what makes the other person unique."

Chapter28

"True love is not about possession, but about mutual respect, trust, and the willingness to let each other be free."

Chapter29

"When you love someone, you become part of something greater than yourself. It's about building a life together and creating a legacy."

Chapter30

"Love is about creating a safe and supportive space where both people can grow, learn, and become the best version of themselves."

Chapter31

"Love is about seeing the other person's soul and connecting with them on a deeper level."

Chapter32

"True love is not just about finding someone who makes you happy, but about finding someone who brings out the best in you."

Chapter33

"When you love someone, you don't just want to be with them, you need to be with them."

Chapter34

"Love is about recognizing the beauty in each other's flaws and embracing them as part of what makes the other person unique."

Chapter35

"True love is not just about finding someone who loves you, but about finding someone who inspires you to love yourself."

Chapter36

"When you love someone, you don't just love them for who they are, but for who they could be with your support and encouragement."

Chapter37

"Love is about being patient, kind, and understanding, even when it's difficult or inconvenient."

Chapter38

"True love is not just about being with someone who makes you happy, but about being with someone who makes you a better person."

Chapter39

"When you love someone, you don't just give them your heart, you give them your trust, loyalty, and commitment."

Chapter40

"Love is about creating a bond that cannot be broken by distance, time, or adversity."

Chapter41

"True love is not about finding someone who completes you, but about finding someone who complements you."

Chapter42

"Love is about finding someone who loves your quirks, your flaws, and your weirdness."

Chapter43

"When you love someone, you don't just want to spend time with them, you want to build a life with them."

Chapter44

"Love is about accepting each other's past, embracing each other's present, and building a future together."

Chapter45

"True love is not just about finding someone who makes you happy, but about finding someone who makes you feel alive."

Chapter46

"When you love someone, you don't just love them for what they are, but for what they could be with your love and support."

Chapter47

Chapter48

"True love is not just about being with someone who shares your interests, but about being with someone who inspires you to try new things and explore new horizons."

Chapter49

"When you love someone, you don't just love them for their successes, but for their struggles and how they overcome them."

Chapter50

"Love is about creating a safe and loving space where both people can be their authentic selves and grow together."

Chapter51

"True love is not just about being with someone who makes you feel good, but about being with someone who makes you feel whole."

Chapter52

"Love is about building a foundation of trust, respect, and communication, that can weather any storm."

Chapter53

"When you love someone, you don't just love the good times, but you also embrace the challenges and grow through them together."

Chapter54

"Love is about seeing the beauty in the ordinary moments of life and finding joy in each other's company."

Chapter55

"True love is not about finding someone who is perfect, but about finding someone who is perfect for you."

Chapter56

"When you love someone, you don't just love them for their strengths, but also for their vulnerabilities and imperfections."

Chapter57

"Love is about creating a partnership that is based on equality, mutual respect, and a shared vision for the future."

Chapter58

"True love is not just about the passion and the romance, but about the deep connection that is forged through time and experience."

Chapter59

"When you love someone, you don't just love them for their physical appearance, but for the beauty that shines from within."

Chapter60

"Love is about supporting each other's dreams and aspirations, and helping each other become the best versions of ourselves."

Chapter61

"True love is not just about being with someone who makes you happy, but about being with someone who challenges you to be your best self."

Chapter62

"Love is about creating a space where two people can grow together, learn from each other, and inspire one another."

Chapter63

"When you love someone, you don't just see their flaws, you see their potential and what they can become with your love and encouragement."

Chapter64

"Love is about creating a bond that is stronger than any obstacle, and a connection that is deeper than any distance."

Chapter65

"True love is not about possessing someone, but about cherishing their individuality and allowing them the freedom to be themselves."

Chapter66

"When you love someone, you don't just love them for their successes, but for the hard work, dedication, and perseverance that got them there."

Chapter67

"Love is about accepting each other's differences, embracing each other's strengths, and helping each other through weaknesses."

Chapter68

"True love is not just about finding someone who shares your interests, but about finding someone who complements you and brings out the best in you."

Chapter69

"When you love someone, you don't just love the good times, but you also cherish the difficult moments because they bring you closer together."

Chapter70

"Love is about creating a partnership that is based on mutual respect, understanding, and a deep appreciation for one another."

Chapter71

"True love is about understanding that love is not always easy, but it is always worth it."

Chapter72

"Love is about creating a safe and nurturing environment where two people can be vulnerable and authentic with one another."

Chapter73

"When you love someone, you don't just love the person they are today, but the person they have the potential to become."

Chapter74

"Love is about being patient and kind, even in the face of difficulty or hardship."

Chapter75

"True love is about creating a connection that is built on honesty, trust, and mutual understanding."

Chapter76

"When you love someone, you don't just love them for the things they do, but for the person they are at their core."

Chapter77

"Love is about creating a relationship that is based on equality, where both people are valued and respected for who they are."

Chapter78

"True love is about finding someone who can be your best friend, your lover, and your partner in all aspects of life."

Chapter79

"When you love someone, you don't just love them for their strengths, but for the vulnerabilities that make them human."

Chapter80

"Love is about embracing each other's flaws and seeing them as opportunities for growth and learning."

Chapter81

"True love is about creating a home in each other's hearts, a place where both people can always feel safe and loved."

Chapter82

"Love is about celebrating each other's achievements and supporting each other through life's challenges."

Chapter83

"When you love someone, you don't just love their good qualities, but you embrace their flaws as part of what makes them unique and beautiful."

Chapter84

"Love is about creating a connection that is built on deep understanding, empathy, and shared values."

Chapter85

"True love is about choosing to love someone, not just when it's easy, but even when it's hard."

Chapter86

"When you love someone, you don't just love them for the happiness they bring you, but for the person they inspire you to become."

Chapter87

"Love is about creating a partnership where both people feel heard, seen, and valued for who they are."

Chapter88

"True love is about being there for each other, not just in the big moments, but in the small ones too."

Chapter89

"When you love someone, you don't just love them for the present, but you look forward to the future you will build together."

Chapter90

"Love is about creating a connection that is based on mutual trust, respect, and a deep appreciation for one another."

Chapter91

"True love is about creating a bond that is unbreakable, even in the face of adversity."

Chapter92

"Love is about creating a connection that is built on open communication, honesty, and vulnerability."

Chapter93

"When you love someone, you don't just love them for their looks, but for the beauty they hold within their heart and soul."

Chapter94

"Love is about creating a partnership that is based on shared values, dreams, and goals."

Chapter95

"True love is about being there for each other, even when it's not easy or convenient."

Chapter96

"When you love someone, you don't just love them for their successes, but for the hard work and determination that got them there."

Chapter97

"Love is about creating a relationship where both people feel supported, encouraged, and inspired to be their best selves."

Chapter98

"True love is about seeing the best in each other, even in the midst of difficult circumstances."

Chapter99

"When you love someone, you don't just love the person they are today, but you love the person they are becoming."

Chapter100

"Love is about creating a connection that is rooted in compassion, kindness, and understanding."

Chapter101

"True love is about making a commitment to each other, to grow and learn together throughout life's journey."

Chapter102

"Love is about creating a connection that is built on mutual respect, admiration, and acceptance."

Chapter103

"When you love someone, you don't just love their strengths, but you love their weaknesses too because that's what makes them human."

Chapter104

"Love is about creating a partnership that is based on shared experiences, memories, and moments of joy."

Chapter105

"True love is about seeing the beauty and potential in each other, even when it's not obvious to anyone else."

Chapter106

"When you love someone, you don't just love the happy moments, but you love them even more in the moments of sadness and struggle."

Chapter107

"Love is about creating a relationship that is based on mutual trust, loyalty, and devotion."

Chapter108

"True love is about celebrating each other's individuality and uniqueness, rather than trying to change each other."

Chapter109

"When you love someone, you don't just love them for their physical appearance, but for the person they are on the inside."

Chapter110

"Love is about creating a connection that is rooted in a deep sense of gratitude and appreciation for each other."

Chapter111

"True love is about building a foundation of trust, respect, and understanding that allows both partners to grow and flourish."

Chapter112

"Love is about finding someone who complements you, challenges you, and supports you in all that you do."

Chapter113

"When you love someone, you don't just love them for their accomplishments, but for the person they are at their core."

Chapter114

"Love is about creating a partnership that is based on deep emotional intimacy, friendship, and a shared sense of purpose."

Chapter115

"True love is about weathering the storms of life together, and emerging stronger and more resilient because of it."

Chapter116

"When you love someone, you don't just love them for their strengths, but you love them for their vulnerabilities too."

Chapter117

"Love is about creating a relationship where both partners feel free to be themselves, and can grow and evolve together over time."

Chapter118

"True love is about finding someone who understands you on a deep level, and accepts you for who you are, flaws and all."

Chapter119

"When you love someone, you don't just love them for their physical appearance, but for the unique qualities that make them who they are."

Chapter120

"Love is about creating a connection that is based on deep trust, mutual respect, and an unbreakable bond."

9 798890 023704

Printed by Libri Plureos GmbH in Hamburg,
Germany